Growing
Through
Arts™

by *Aleksandra* ℠

# THE Nutcracker BALLET

BY *Aleksandra* SM

BALLET SERIES

Growing Through Arts

ORCHID PUBLISHING | CHICAGO

Illustrations by Elizaveta Efimova

Special Thanks to Russian Pointe Dance Boutique, Joffrey Ballet, Scott Speck, Auditorium Theatre of Roosevelt
University, River North Dance Company and Vala Dancewear for Glossary photos.

Library of Congress Control Number: 2010918292
ISBN 978-0-9831641-0-4

Production Date: January 20, 2011
Printing Plant Location: Everbest Printing Co. Ltd.,
    Nansha, China
Job/Batch #: EPC-RN-97951.4 R4

What do ballet, art, and music have to do with leadership, academic achievement, and career success? A lot, it turns out.

Growing up in St. Petersburg, Russia, I was immersed in the arts. I saw astounding performances at the Kirov Ballet, art masterpieces at the Hermitage State Museum, world-renown operas and breathtaking European architecture. Little did I know back then what a profound effect the arts would have on my life. But now, as an adult who is actively involved in international business, education, and community service, the impact is clear: My background in the arts plays a vital part in every facet of my life.

That's why I'm bringing **Growing Through Arts**™ to you and your family. My goal is to make your children curious and excited about dance, music, and visual art, to inspire them to participate in the arts and learn more about them. Involvement in the creative arts develops key strengths in children—discipline, teamwork, confidence, aesthetic judgment, and pride in achievement, just to name a few—that enrich their lives immeasurably and lay the groundwork for success in *all* areas of life.

As a dancer, I know the thrill of sharing the passion of ballet with an audience. Now I want to share the enchanting world of ballet with your family.

**Growing Through Arts**™ teaches children that with vision, commitment, study, and practice, they can not only achieve all of their dreams but go far beyond them. May the ideas and values offered here play a small part in raising strong, passionate, and talented individuals and leaders.

Ever Growing Through Arts,
Aleksandra

# How to Use This Book

- Read the story to your child many times to encourage memory and to explore the themes more deeply.

- Pretend you're in a theater, watching the "ballet" unfold on stage!

- Read and discuss Miss Aleksandra's Themes & Values, integrated throughout the book, and look for ways to relate them to your child's life.

- At the end of the book, use Miss Aleksandra's Glossary to learn the new vocabulary words introduced in the story and to enjoy beautiful photo illustrations of ballet concepts.

- Engage in a thoughtful dialogue with your child—ask questions about the story, pictures, and characters.

- Expand your fun and learning time with your child by doing activities in the Practice & Play book (sold separately), which integrates characters and story elements from the storybook.

Hurry, let's take our seats, the **ballet** is about to begin! We're going to watch *The Nutcracker*, by the famous Russian **composer,** Peter Ilyich Tchaikovsky.

Listen, the music is starting! Look, the **stage** lights come aglow! The **curtains** whisk apart. A spectacular **set** sparkles with light. Now the dancers begin to move and the magic of the story sweeps us away . . .

The Holidays had come to Clara's home. Piles of presents circled the tree and the smell of cider filled the air. Everyone laughed and sang as family and friends poured in from the snowy street to join the celebration.

Clara sat by herself in a corner. She was a quiet girl who loved to play pretend games with her toys.

"Quiet Clara, shy as a mouse!" teased her brother Fritz. "Telling silly stories in her head!" The other children laughed. Clara felt hurt but didn't say a word. And when Fritz grabbed her mouse toy and ran away, she didn't try to stop him.

MISS Aleksandra's
THEMES & VALUES

*Are the children in this scene showing respect and kindness to someone who is different from them? What do you think about that?*

"Look who's here!" someone shouted. It was Herr Drosselmeyer! He was Clara's Godfather and a very clever toymaker. Every year he brought special surprises to the holiday party. The children gathered around him as he slid a huge box from his toy sack and popped it open.

Out jumped two life-size dolls! They pranced and danced about the room, enchanting everyone. In Clara's mind they told a whole story with their dance steps. She wished the story would never end!

*Dance can inspire our imagination!*

"I think I *might* have brought a few presents, too," said Herr Drosselmeyer. He handed out gifts to all the boys and girls. There were dress-up dolls and wonderful wooden puzzles. Clara quietly waited her turn as all the children opened their gifts. Fritz got a toy pony to ride! "I guess that's the last one," said Herr Drosselmeyer, closing up his sack.

MISS
*Aleksandra's*
THEMES &
VALUES

*What quality is Clara showing when she quietly waits her turn without complaining? (Patience)*

12

Clara had been forgotten. She wanted to cry, but she didn't say a word. "Wait, what's this?" said Herr Drosselmeyer, reaching in his sack one last time. Out came a brightly colored nutcracker, painted like a soldier. He handed it to Clara. "This one is for you, my shy dear."

"Thank you, thank you!"  said Clara. She loved her nutcracker more than any toy she'd ever seen! The moment she touched it, she imagined it coming to life and . . .

MISS *Aleksandra's*
THEMES &
VALUES

*What is the polite thing to say when you receive a gift? Why?*

"Give me that!" shouted Fritz. "Your present's better than mine." He grabbed the nutcracker and ran toward the door.

"STOP!" shouted Clara in a big booming voice.  "YOU CAN'T HAVE HIM!" The whole room went quiet. No one had ever heard Clara speak this way.

Fritz threw the nutcracker and it hit the floor with a loud *crack*! Clara gasped in horror. Her toy was broken.

*When you see someone doing something wrong, should you speak up or stay quiet?*

She bandaged the nutcracker with a cloth and placed it in a tiny bed beneath the tree. All evening long, as the other children ate holiday sweets, Clara cared for her nutcracker.

"I'm sorry," said Fritz at last. "I didn't mean to break it."

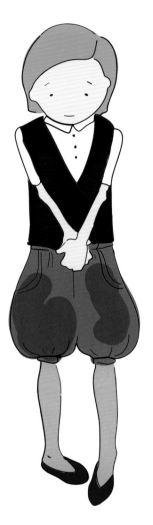

MISS *Aleksandra's*
THEMES & VALUES

*When others are hurt or sick, how should you treat them?*

*When you do something wrong to someone, what is the next thing you should do? (Apologize. Also, try to make things better.)*

When all the guests had left and her family had gone to bed, Clara crept downstairs to check on her nutcracker one last time. "I wish for you to be healed," she whispered. "I'd give up sweets *forever* to make that happen."

At that moment, the tree began to *grow*! Or was Clara getting smaller? Yes, she shrunk to the size of a toy!

She rubbed her eyes and suddenly a huge mouse appeared before her, standing on two feet and dressed in the robes of a king. He was dancing a scary dance, with a whole army of mice behind him.

*Being unselfish means being willing to give up something of your own to help someone else.*

Clara was frightened and wanted to run. But her nutcracker marched up behind her with an army of tin soldiers. "I'm here to help," he said.

A battle began! The nutcracker fought bravely, but the mouse army was too powerful. The mice grabbed the nutcracker and tried to carry him away.

"STOP!" shouted Clara, just as she had at Fritz. "YOU CAN'T HAVE HIM!" Then she threw the only thing she could find—her **slipper**!—at the mouse king. Instantly, the whole mouse army disappeared! Clara didn't know what to think.

MISS *Aleksandra's* THEMES & VALUES

*What should you do when you see someone being picked on by others?*

"Your courage broke an evil spell!" explained the nutcracker, who changed into a handsome prince before her eyes. "You've made the whole world sweet again. Come see!"

*What does it mean to have courage?*
*Why do you think Clara is rewarded for her courage?*

The prince and Clara danced into a sleigh, then off they flew through a glittering winter garden of snowflake ballerinas . . .

Look! The stage lights dim and the curtains close. **Act** 1 is over.
The **audience** can stretch and take a break. Soon the stage lights
go up and the curtains open again. Act 2 begins!

The sleigh carried Clara all the way to the Kingdom of Sweets, a luscious land of tasty treats. Everywhere she looked were gumdrops and ice cream sundaes and cake palaces covered in frosting. A Sugar Plum Fairy danced before her, placing a crown on Clara's head. "Thank you for making all this happen," she said.

MISS *Aleksandra's* THEMES & VALUES

There's "magic" in being unselfish. Clara passes up sweets so she can take care of her nutcracker. But then she is rewarded with a whole kingdom of sweets!

22

A special **performance** was put on just for Clara. She held her breath as dancers from all over the world leapt and spun in splendid **costumes**. She watched a Spanish cocoa dance, an Arabian coffee dance, and a Chinese tea dance. Dancers from Russia scurried about like little *Matryoshka* dolls!

*All cultures of the world have something beautiful to offer, don't you think?*

Mother Ginger appeared next. She wore a giant dress that filled the whole stage! When she lifted it up, out danced joyous Gingerbread Children!

Next the flower fairies danced in tiny **tutus** and the Sugar Plum Fairy performed magnificently. "Bravo!" shouted Clara. "Bravo!"

Clara turned to the Prince and said, "I wish this night would never end."

"It never will," said the Prince, "if you have the imagination to keep it alive."

"I do," said Clara, feeling surer of herself than ever before. "I do."

Clara opened her eyes and found herself beneath the tree the next morning. Her family was all around her and she held the nutcracker gently in her arms. When she looked at it, the crack was gone! "He's all better, just like I imagined he would be!"

*Did Clara really go to the Kingdom of Sweets or did she only imagine it? Did her wishing heal the nutcracker or did Herr Drosselmeyer fix it? Stories don't always give us an answer; sometimes they let us decide for ourselves!*

"You must have a very powerful imagination," winked Herr Drosselmeyer, who had come by to check on Clara.

"I do," said Clara proudly. "And I'm going to share it with everyone."

"What do you mean?" asked her mom.

"My stories aren't silly; they're magical. And I'm going to tell *more* of them. I'm going to tell stories full of dancing and music and magic."

"Well," her mom replied, "perhaps one day you'll be a **choreographer.** You can do for audiences what you did for your nutcracker."

"Really?" said Clara. Her eyes grew wide as she thought about all the amazing stories she could tell with dance.

*Clara learns to speak up for herself and to believe in her imagination. What a great combination!*

"With your imagination," said her father, "you can do anything you want."

"I know," said Clara, hugging her nutcracker tightly. "I know."

*When you picture a goal in your mind and work hard for it, anything is possible!*

And now the curtains close, the lights go down, and the last note of music plays. As the audience leaves, the theater goes dark and quiet . . .

But don't worry. Tomorrow the dance will begin again and the magic will live once more!

# Glossary

COURTESY RUSSIAN POINTE DANCE BOUTIQUE

**audience**

COURTESY RUSSIAN POINTE DANCE BOUTIQUE

**costume**

A ballet is sometimes divided into parts called **acts**. Between acts, the curtain closes and the stage lights go down.

The **audience** is the group of people who come to see a show. They sit in the seats and face the stage.

**Ballet** is an elegant style of classical dancing. "*A* ballet" is a performance in which music and dance come together to tell a story.

The **choreographer** arranges the movements for the dancers. It's the choreographer's job to decide *how* a story will be told in dance.

The **composer** writes the music for a ballet.

A **costume** is the special clothing that helps a dancer create a character. Some costumes are beautiful, some are frightening or funny.

The **curtain** is a large piece of cloth that hides the stage from the audience before and after a performance.

A show put on by dancers or other performing artists is called a **performance**.

A **set** is the furniture, walls, and decorations that come together to create a *scene* on stage.

A **slipper** is a light shoe used for ballet dancing.

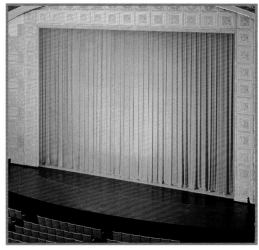

curtain

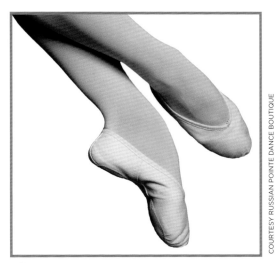

slipper

**stage**

**theater**

**tutu**

The **stage** is the area where dancers, singers, and actors perform for an audience.

A **theater** is a building that has a stage and seats for an audience. People go to a theater to watch a ballet.

A **tutu** is the short, beautiful skirt a ballerina wears as part of her costume.

# ABOUT *Aleksandra* ℠

**Aleksandra Efimova** is the founder of **Growing Through Arts**™ and President of Russian Pointe, Inc., a brand of luxury ballet shoes with a flagship boutique on Chicago's Magnificent Mile. Born in St. Petersburg, Russia, Aleksandra graduated from the renowned Art School at the Hermitage State Art Museum and received training in classical dance, art, and academics. In 1993, she moved to United States, where she started her first successful company while still an undergraduate student. An alumna of Harvard Business School, she is an inspirational speaker and writer and is actively involved in promoting the arts, international collaboration, and education in the community.

## OTHER BOOKS IN
## THE GROWING THROUGH ARTS™

### BALLET SERIES

*The Cinderella Ballet* by Aleksandra[SM] (storybook)

*The Sleeping Beauty Ballet* by Aleksandra[SM] (storybook)

*The Nutcracker Ballet Practice & Play Book* by Aleksandra[SM]

*The Cinderella Ballet Practice & Play Book* by Aleksandra[SM]

*The Sleeping Beauty Ballet Practice & Play Book* by Aleksandra[SM]

### MUSIC SERIES

*The Peter and the Wolf Symphony* by Aleksandra[SM] (storybook)

*The Snow Maiden Opera* by Aleksandra[SM] (storybook)

*Twist, A Musical* by Aleksandra[SM] (storybook)

*The Peter and the Wolf Symphony Practice & Play Book* by Aleksandra[SM]

*The Snow Maiden Opera Practice & Play Book* by Aleksandra[SM]

*Twist, A Musical Practice & Play Book* by Aleksandra[SM]

hrough Art

rough Art &
Gro

Growing Thro